1 MONTH OF
FREE
READING

at

www.ForgottenBooks.com

By purchasing this book you are eligible for one month membership to ForgottenBooks.com, giving you unlimited access to our entire collection of over 1,000,000 titles via our web site and mobile apps.

To claim your free month visit:

www.forgottenbooks.com/free1303162

ISBN 978-0-428-68125-8
PIBN 11303162

SIXTEENTH

ANNUAL ANNOUNCEMENT

OF

Columbus Medical College

OF

COLUMBUS, OHIO.

SESSION OF 1890-91.

Regular Session opens Wednesday, September 3d,
1890, and Closes Thursday, March 5th, 1891.

COLUMBUS
PRESS OF THE OHIO STATE JOURNAL
1890

CALENDAR FOR THE TERM.

Course begins Wednesday, September 3d, 1890.

Holiday Vacation begins Saturday, December 20th, 1890.

Course resumed Monday, January 5th, 1891.

Legal Holidays are observed.

Examination for Matriculation Tuesday, September 2d, 1890.

Examinations for Degree will begin on Monday, February 23d, 1891.

Graduation Exercises will be held Thursday, March 5th, 1891.

SPRING COURSE.

Course begins Wednesday, March 11th, 1891.

Course closes May 20th, 1891.

FACULTY.

J. W. HAMILTON, A.M., M.D., 142 East Long Street,
Professor of Surgery, Clinical Surgery.

H. C. PEARCE, A.M., M.D., Ph.D., Urbana, Ohio,
Professor of Obstetrics and Surgical Diseases of Women.

D. N. KINSMAN, M.D., 215 East Town Street,
Professor of Theory and Practice of Medicine and Clinical Medicine, and Dean of the Faculty.

E. H. HYATT, M.D., Delaware, Ohio,
Professor of Materia Medica and Therapeutics.

J. M. DUNHAM, A.M., M.D., 222 East Town Street,
Professor of Diseases of Women and Children, Clinical Medicine, and Secretary of the Faculty.

JOSIAH MEDBERY, A.M., M.D., 35 East Chestnut Street,
Professor of Anatomy, and Registrar.

GEORGE M. WATERS, M.D., 1272 North High Street,
Professor of Physiology and Physiological Anatomy.

FRANCIS W. BLAKE, A.M., M.D., 33 South Fourth Street,
Professor of Chemistry, and Lecturer on Rhinology and Laryngology.

W. D. HAMILTON, A.B., M.D., 142 East Long Street,
Demonstrator of Anatomy and Adjunct to Chair of Surgery.

N. R. COLEMAN, M.D., 264 East Town Street,
Professor of Physical Diagnosis.

HARLAN P. ALLEN, M.D., 73 East State Street,
Professor of Ophthalmology and Otology.

M. F. LEE, M.D.,
Professor of Venereal Diseases and Dermatology.

Professor of Medical Jurisprudence.

J. U. BARNHILL, A.M., M.D., 188 East Town Street,
Adjunct Professor of Materia Medica and Therapeutics.

C. S. HAMILTON, A.B., M.D.,
Lecturer on Pathological Anatomy and Demonstrator of Microscopy.

OTTO ARNOLD, D.D.S., 62 East Broad Street,
Lecturer on Dental Surgery.

SAMUEL IGLICK, M.D.,
Assistant to Chair of Anatomy.

J. E. BROWN, B.S., M.D.,
Assistant to Chair of Obstetrics.

ANNOUNCEMENT.

THE year just passed has been one of unusual encouragement. A spirit of enthusiasm and earnest effort pervaded the work of both students and Faculty. We look forward to the coming year's work with increased confidence in our ability to offer more inducements to students, and accomplish better results in equiping men for the practice of our profession than ever before.

The conscientious and thorough work we have ever endeavored to perform is bearing its fruit in the high standing taken by our alumni. To this announcement we have appended a list of our graduates, to whom reference can be made regarding the character of instruction they received at this institution.

It will be our aim to keep abreast with the most enlightened methods of imparting medical instruction, and in every way retain the confidence so freely extended to us by our friends in the profession. For several years past we have *earnestly recommended* a three years' graded course, and would now make the announcement that, beginning with the term of 1892–3, we will require that all candidates for graduation shall have attended three full courses of lectures.

Columbus is centrally located, and easily accessible from every direction. It has considerably above one hundred thousand inhabitants and is rapidly increasing in population. The cost of living is moderate. Clinical advantages are enhanced by the location of five large State institutions in our midst. Our clinics hold tributary a large population in Central Ohio contiguous to the city. Clinical instructions is given regularly during the term at Hawkes' Hospital, and at the Hospital of the Ohio Penitentiary.

ANATOMY.

In the Department of Osteology our mode of instruction is peculiar; and our large Cabinet, which includes twenty-five skeletons, supplies the means of making it effective. At the beginning of each lecture specimens are distributed in the class, so that every squad of three or four students is supplied with the bone under discussion. Every student is thus enabled to familiarize himself with the points of each bone by seeing and handling it. The Course in Osteology consists of about twenty-five lectures. The remainder of the course, about seventy lectures, is devoted to the soft parts, and is demonstrated upon the cadaver.

PRACTICAL ANATOMY.

The Dissecting Room will not be opened until the class is well drilled in Osteology. It possesses rare adaptation to its purpose. Every table will be supplied with thoroughly injected material. This preparation is indispensable to the accuracy which we require; and only such work will be accredited by the Demonstrator, or accepted by the Faculty. In this connection it is proper to state that it has always been the practice of the institution to require THREE FULL DISSECTIONS, which embrace the entire human body. Students should be provided with a good dissector.

CHEMISTRY.

The Course in Chemistry will consist of two lectures per week. In connection with which, students will receive practical instruction under the supervision of the Demonstrator, in chemical manipulations, including the detection of poisons, urinalysis, and such other work as the practitioner may be called upon to perform.

Laboratory work is indispensable in the pursuit of this branch of study, and at least as much time will be given to it as to the lectures.

All candidates for graduation will be required to take this practical course.

PHYSIOLOGY.

Lectures on Physiology, while embracing the discussion of the advanced theories of the science, are made eminently practical, and are abundantly illustrated by drawings, microscopic exhibitions, and numerous experiments on living animals. Three lectures and a quiz will be given each week throughout the term.

The Physiological Anatomy and Physiology of the Nervous System will be taught from a practical standpoint and in direct relation to nervous diseases, and made especially interesting and instructive by vivisections, blackboard illustrations and clinical lectures.

MATERIA MEDICA.

Our Cabinet collection in Materia Medica is large and well selected. It embraces a full line of crude drugs, vegetable alkaloids, organic and inorganic salts, resinoids, extracts, etc. This will serve to familiarize the student with the physical characteristics of drugs as they reach the practitioner, and afford ready means of determining their purity and detecting adulterations.

To enable the student to better understand this important branch of study, the following topics will be discussed relative to medicines in general use by the profession:

1. Their natural history and physical characteristics.
2. Physiological actions.
3. Therapeutic application.

4. Toxicology, and methods of treatment.
5. Physiological antagonisms.
6. Incompatibles.

Instructions will be given in prescription writing.

The principles of Electro-Therapeutics are also elucidated.

SURGERY.

In this department a systematic and thorough course is given, consisting of four or five didactic lectures per week. Surgical proceedures are taught, as far as possible, by demonstrations, which are of the most varied character. Examinations, written and oral, cover all the topics taught.

OBSTETRICS.

In the Department of Obstetrics the teaching will be practical. The various operations, and the use of the instruments, will be illustrated, and the student taught to perform the same upon the manikin. So far as possible, each candidate will be given an opportunity to assist or conduct a case of labor.

DISEASES OF WOMEN AND CHILDREN.

The Department of Gynecology will be thoroughly taught, both in theory and practice, and all instruments and other appliances required in treating the diseases of females will be presented, and students will be instructed in the use of the speculum, probe and digital touch as aids to diagnosis.

Preliminary lectures will be given on Pathology, the peculiarities of organization and function incident to childhood, and the diet and laws of hygiene of that period. The course will include the diseases of infancy and childhood.

THEORY AND PRACTICE OF MEDICINE.

Four hours will be devoted to didactic and two hours to clinical instruction, weekly, by the Professor of Practice. In addition, courses are given on Physical Diagnosis, Medical Jurisprudence, Cutaneous Diseases and Hygiene, by the respective professors of these departments.

OPHTHALMOLOGY AND OTOLOGY.

About forty didactic and clinical lectures are delivered on these subjects, especial attention being given to the diseases of the more superficial parts, which the general practitioner must be able to recognize and treat; and to the relation of eye and ear changes to general diseases. Rapid strides have been made in these branches in the past few years, and they now constitute an important part of every medical curriculum. The facilities of the College for didactic instruction are excellent, and the advantages offered by the Hawkes Hospital and Ohio Penitentiary for clinical teaching are unsurpassed. The free quiz will be continued.

RHINOLOGY AND LARYNGOLOGY.

Lectures on these topics will include the special anatomy and pathology of the parts, with demonstration of the practical use of the instruments applied to the examination and treatment of the nose and larynx.

HISTOLOGY AND PATHOLOGY.

A laboratory course in microscopic work is provided ; and the College has an equipment of microscopes of modern and approved construction for the use of students.

Practical instruction is given in the technical proceedures of section cutting, staining and mounting.

Lectures are also given upon the principles underlying this most important department of medical study.

The pursuit of this practical work is made a requirement for graduation.

AMONG OUR MEANS OF ILLUSTRATION ARE

A Museum, containing an extensive list of wet and dry preparations, illustrating almost every variety of surgical disease; the *papier mache* anatomical preparations of Ramme and Saldtmann, of Hamburg; a complete set of Prof. Bock's Anatomical Models; an Osteological Cabinet of twenty-five complete human skeletons; an oxy-hydrogen lantern, with transparencies for use therewith.

Microscopes and an extensive cabinet of microscopic slides, serve to illustrate normal and morbid histology.

CLINICS.

SURGICAL CLINICS.

The Saturday morning clinic, in the College, as now arranged, brings to it a large proportion of the commoner surgical diseases, deformities and accidents, and is an exceptionally rich field for the study of these cases and the manifold treatment and dressings applicable to each. The graver operations are performed in the amphitheatre of the Hawkes Hospital.

HAWKES HOSPITAL.

J. W. HAMILTON, M. D.,
Consulting Surgeon.

D. N. KINSMAN, M. D.,
Consulting Physician.

N. R. COLEMAN, M. D.,
Diseases of the Chest.

H. P. ALLEN, M. D.,
Diseases of the Eye and Ear.

F. W. BLAKE, M. D.,
Diseases of Throat and Nose.

J. M. DUNHAM, M. D.,
Diseases of Women and Children.

M. F. LEE, M. D.,
Genito Urinary and Skin Diseases.

GEO. M. WATERS, M. D.,
Nervous and Mental Diseases.

W. D. HAMILTON, M. D.,
General Surgery.

J. U. BARNHILL, M. D.
General Medicine.

C. S. HAMILTON, M. D.,
General Surgery, Pathologist.

This institution was founded by money and land deeded to the Columbus Medical College by the late Dr. W. B. Hawkes, of the Board of Trustees. The capacity of the building first erected has, in less than four years, proved inadequate, and an additional building is about to be constructed which will allow of more than double the number of beds. At present there are ample accommodations for one hundred patients. The equipments, including elevators, furnishings, fire protection, etc., are of the best. Every facility for clinical instruction is provided for the student.

THIS HOSPITAL IS OWNED BY AND UNDER THE CONTROL OF THE COLUMBUS MEDICAL COLLEGE. Clinics of every character are given here one-half day each week, besides numerous extra cases as emergencies arise.

Although it has been in operation less than four years, yet the work performed has far exceeded that of many of the older hospitals throughout the country, as the appended summary of some of the more important operations during the past session will show.

Operations upon the Genito-Urinary Organs and Rectum 51
Abdominal operations... 23
Operations upon the bones and joints 22
Operations upon the eye 15
Amputations of breast 10

MEDICAL CLINICS.

A clinic is given weekly in the Hospital of the Ohio Penitentiary. The convict population varies from thirteen to sixteen hundred, and affords a rich field for clinical demonstration.

Clinics are also held at Hawkes Hospital, and before the class in the College.

PRELIMINARY REQUIREMENTS FOR MATRICULATION.

Matriculants must give evidence of a fair English education, as shown by diplomas from Colleges, High Schools or Normal Schools, certificates for teaching, or other satisfactory evidence.

Candidates not so provided will present themselves for examination in the Museum Room, at the College, on Tuesday, Sept. 2d, at 10 A. M.

Hereafter no women will be admitted.

FEES.

Matriculation, each term	$ 5 00
Tickets, first course of lectures	40 00
" second "	40 00
" third "	20 00
Examination Fee, for graduation	25 00
Demonstrator of Anatomy	5 00
Demonstrator of Chemistry	5 00
Hospital Ticket	Free.

☞ Matriculation and Term Fees must be paid at time of entrance.

REQUIREMENTS FOR GRADUATION.

The candidate must have studied three years under the direction of a regular practitioner of medicine. He must have attended not less than two courses of lectures, the last being at this College. He must have attended one course of clinical lectures at the Hospital. He must have made one complete dissection of the human body. He must have pursued laboratory courses in Chemistry and Pathology. He must pass a satisfactory examination in each of the following branches, viz : Chemistry, Anatomy, Physiology, Materia Medica and Therapeutics, Obstetrics, Gynecology, Surgery and Practice of Medicine. He must write and defend a thesis upon some subject relating to medicine or surgery. He must be twenty-one years of age, and exhibit testimonials of good moral character (blanks for which will be furnished). All his certificates must be full and explicit.

TEXT BOOKS.

One or more of the following text books are recommended in each of the departments. These books can be procured in Columbus at the usual student's discount prices.

Anatomy—Gray, Wilson, Ellis, Darling, Ranney, Weisse.

Dissector—Heath's Practical Anatomy.

Physiology—Landois, Kirke, Dalton, Foster.

Obstetrics—Leishman, Playfair, Lusk, Galabin.

Surgery—Ashurst, Gross, Bryant, Druitt, Wyeth.

Practice—Flint, Bartholow, Loomis, Strumpfell.

Physical Diagnosis—Loomis, Da Costa, Flint.

Materia Medica—H. C. Wood, Headland, Ringer, Nat'l Dispensatory, Lauder Brunton, Biddle.

Gynecology—Thomas, Barnes, Emmett.

Ophthalmology—Nettleship, Swanzy, Noyes.

Otology—Burnett, Roosa, Buck (Edition of '89).

Chemistry—Simon, Bloxam, Bartley, Draper's Laboratory Guide.

Diseases of Children—Smith, Goodhart, Tanner, Day.

Pathology—Delafield and Prudden, Paine, Billroth.

Nervous System—Ross, Gowers, Bramwell.

Jurisprudence—Wharton and Stillé, Taylor, Reese.

Venereal—Van Buren and Keyes, Bumstead and Taylor.

Dermatology—Duhring, Fox, Anderson.

Histology—Prudden.

Rhinology and Laryngology—Sajous, Bosworth.

PRIZES.

The Faculty of Columbus Medical College offers the following prizes for 1890–91:

First prize	$100 00
Second prize	60 00
Third prize	40 00

CONDITIONS.

The six students who shall attain the highest average grades in the general examination for graduation, by all the chairs, shall be admitted to a competitive examination in the branches of Chemistry, Anatomy, Physiology, Materia Medica, Obstetrics, Surgery, Gynecology and the Practice of Medicine; and they shall be entitled to the prizes and honorable mention in the order of their grades, as determined by their papers. The examination shall be conducted by a committee of the Faculty, in such a manner that the authors of the several papers shall be unknown until after the final decision.

THE PRIZES OF 1889-90

Were awarded as follows: 1st prize, $50.00, to A. E. Lawrence; 2d prize, $40.00, to G. A. Phillips; 3d prize, $30.00, to C. W. Chidester; 4th prize, $20.00, to C. S. McCafferty.

Those receiving honorable mention were: F. M. Macklin, A. B. Davenport, C. L. Rosengrant, J. C. Bowman.

SPECIAL PRIZES.

In addition to the Faculty Prizes, just mentioned, the following are offered by individual members of the Faculty.

For the best examination in *Physical Diagnosis*, Professor Coleman offers a Camman's Stethoscope.

For the best examination in the *Practice of Medicine*, Professor Kinsman offers a set of instruments of precision used in physical diagnosis.

For the best examination in *Ophthalmology and Otology*, Professor Allen offers the latest edition of a treatise on the eye.

A SPRING COURSE.

On Wednesday, March 11th, 1891, will be instituted a regular Spring course of instruction.

It is intended to supplement the work of the regular course by the consideration of important topics in detail; and, by recitations from standard works, to inculcate critical habits of study. Clinical demonstrations will diversify the work as opportunity offers.

The course will continue ten weeks. The fee will be $10.00, which will be a credit on the succeeding regular Winter course.

This work is in charge of a Special Faculty, consisting of

T. W. RANKIN, M. D.,	H. M. W. MOORE, A. M., M. D.,
SAMUEL IGLICK,, M. D.,	J. E. BROWN, M. D.,
	P. B. DRISCOLL, M. D.

For further information regarding this course communication should be had with

DR. J. E. BROWN,
108 North Fourth St., COLUMBUS, OHIO.

For other information, address

D. N. KINSMAN, M. D., *Dean*,
215 East Town Street,
COLUMBUS, OHIO.

GRADUATES OF 1890.

BIRMINGHAM, J. W...Ohio.
BOWMAN, J. C...Ohio.
BOWMAN, J. H...Ohio.
BRATTAIN, G. M...Ohio.
BURNS, E. E...Ohio.
CHIDESTER, C. W., B. S....... ....Ohio.
CLARK, A. B...Ohio.
CLOUSE, G. M ....Ohio.
DAVENPORT, A. B...Ohio.
DICKIE, A. D..Pennsylvania.
ELDER, J. T ....Ohio.
HARTMAN, H. H...:Ohio.
JACKSON, W. L...Ohio.
JAMES, H. S...Ohio.
LAWRENCE, A. E..Ohio.
MCCAFFERTY, C. S..Ohio.
MCCAREY, M. J., B. S....................................Pennsylvania.
MCKITRICK, LLEWELLYN ....Ohio.
MACKLIN, F. M ....Ohio.
MAUK, P. P ....Ohio.
MURPHY, J. A ....Ohio.
OLMSTEAD, W. H ....Pennsylvania.
PARKER, C. M ....Ohio.
PEARCE, H. M..Ohio.
PHILLIPS, G. A..Ohio.
ROSENGRANT, C. L..Ohio.
SCOTT, W. C...Ohio.
SHAW, O. J..Ohio.
STALLARD, H. H..Virginia.
YOUNG, H. H...Ohio.

MATRICULANTS FOR 1889-90.

NAME.	STATE.	PRECEPTOR.
Baker, W. G	Ohio	J. U. Barnhill, M. D.
Birmingham, J. W	Ohio	W. T. Rowles, M. D.
Bolon, C. C.	Ohio	Columbus Med. College.
Borman, F. H	Ohio	Columbus Med. College.
Bowman, J. C	Ohio	D. E. Bowman. M. D.
Bowman, J. H	Ohio	D. E. Bowman, M. D.
Bown, H. H	Ohio	F. A. Vigor, M. D.
Brattain, G. M	Ohio	G. E. Brattain, M. D.
Brown, W. H., A. B	Ohio	R. S. Barton, M. D.
Buck, A. H	Ohio	C. C. Dunham, M. D.
Burns, E. E	Ohio	S. H. Yeater, M. D.
Callinan, D. F., jr.	Ohio	G. M. Waters, M. D.
Chidester, C. W., B. S	Ohio	H. G. Campbell, M. D.
Clark, A. B.	Ohio	J. M. Dunham, M. D.
Clouse, G. M	Ohio	H. Hendrixson, M. D.
Criswell, D. M.	Ohio	A. E. Walker, M. D.
Davenport, A. B.	Ohio	Columbus Med. College.
Dennison, A. N., A. B.	Ohio	W. D. Hamilton, M. D.
Dickie, A. D	Indiana	Thos. St. Clair, M. D.
Dombaugh, R. S	Ohio	L. D. Hamilton, M. D.
Dupler, W. P.	Ohio	Columbus Med. College.
Elder, J. T	Ohio	L. A. Harper, M. D.
Gaines, C. E., Ph.B	Ohio	G. M. Waters, M. D.
Geer, N. M	Ohio	W. H. Stokes, M. D.
Hancock, D. R	Ohio	D. N. Kinsman, M. D.
Hart, W. S	Ohio	G. W. Blakeley, M. D.
Hartman, H. H	Ohio	C. L. Coyle, M. D.
Hawk, B. F	Ohio	H. F. McCoy, M. D.
Hawk, P. W	Ohio	H. F. McCoy, M. D.
Henry, J. L	Ohio	R. M. Steele, M. D.
Hughey, R. M	Ohio	B. Hughey, M. D.
Hunter, J. A., A.B	Ohio	Columbus Med. College.
Jackson, W. L	Ohio	A. L. Jackson, M. D.
James, H. S	Ohio	J. W. Johnson, M. D.
Johnson, F. W	Ohio	L. T. Guerin, M. D.
Lawrence, A. E	Ohio	L. A. Harper, M. D.
Lepley, G. C	Ohio	J. P. Strouse. M. D.
McCafferty, C. S	Ohio	D. N. Kinsman, M. D.
McCarey, M. J., B.S	Pennsylvania	J. K. Tretton, M. D.
McKitrick, L	Ohio	A. J. Pounds, M. D.

NAME.	STATE.	PRECEPTOR.
McLaughlin, Oscar	Ohio	J. F. Morgan, M. D.
Macklin, F. M	Ohio	Wm. Warner, M. D.
Manley, C. S., A.B.	Colorado	C. S. Hamilton, M. D.
Mansfield, M. L	Ohio	L. A. Harper, M. D.
Mauk, P. P	Ohio	E. B. Mauk, M. D.
Means, C. S.	Ohio	W. J. Means, M. D.
Murphy, J. A	Ohio	Columbus Med. College.
Olmstead, W. H	Pennsylvania	J. C. Olmstead, M. D.
Parker, C. A.	Ohio	H. G. Campbell, M. D.
Pearce, H. M	Ohio	H. C. Pearce, M. D.
Phillips, G. A	Ohio	T. S. Rosengrant, M. D.
Pilcher, F. N	Ohio	G. W. Blakeley, M. D.
Rauschkolb, Chas	Ohio	Columbus Med. College.
Riegel, F. L	Ohio	Dennis Whittaker, M.D.
Rosengrant, C. L	Ohio	T. S. Rosengrant, M. D.
Sager, T. M	Ohio	C. F. Sager, M. D.
Scott, W. C.	Ohio	E. A. Frampton, M. D.
Shaeffer, J. H	Ohio	R. C. Hoover, sr., M. D.
Shaw, O. J.	Ohio	G. W. Blakeley, M. D.
Shirkey, U. S. L	Ohio	L. McCollum, M. D.
Snyder, D. J., M.A	Ohio	Columbus Med. College.
Stallard, H. H	Virginia	L. L. Banner, M. D.
Stewart, D. G.	Ohio	D. Hudson, M. D.
Stump, E. H	West Virginia	Columbus Med. College.
Tyler, J. A	Ohio	G. M. Waters, M. D.
Vail, H. B	Ohio	A. E. Walker, M. D.
Watson, W. V.	Ohio	J. Bloomfield, M. D.
Williams, F. A	Ohio	Columbus Med. College.
Wood, H. W., B.S.	Illinois	O. P. Hendrixson, M. D.
Wyland, Fred	Ohio	Columbus Med. College.
Young, H. H	Ohio	O. H. Hunt, M. D.

ALUMNI ASSOCIATION.

OFFICERS FOR 1890-91.

President...........................H. S. PRESTON, M. D., Mutual, Ohio.
Vice President ....W. D. HAMILTON, M. D., Columbus, Ohio.
Secretary.........................WM. WHITTEN, M. D., Columbus, Ohio.
Treasurer ....JOSIAH MEDBERY, Columbus, Ohio.

The annual Banquet to the Alumni Association was held on the evening of March 4, after the graduating exercises. A large number were present and passed a most enjoyable evening. We owe much to our *Alma Mater*, and she, in turn, watches our progress with interest, and is ever ready to extend a hearty welcome to all who can avail themselves of this yearly reunion. At our last meeting it was determined to make these gatherings not only interesting in a general way, but also of real improvement to those who attend. A programme is being carefully prepared, and will be announced before the next meeting in '91·

The reputation of an institution rests with its Alumni. The Alumni obtain credit from the prominence of an institution. Their interests are mutual; and it is both our duty and privilege to unite in earnest effort to further the advancement of our College. We want every Alumnus to interest himself actively in the affairs of this Association, and to feel that by so doing he is benefiting both himself and others.

If you change your address please notify the Secretary.

It is earnestly desired to hold a reunion of *all* the members of the classes from 1876 to 1880, inclusive, next March. Please note this meeting in your engagement book for March 4, 1891, and then keep it.

WM. WHITTEN, M. D., SEC'Y,
205 East Rich Street, Columbus, Ohio.

GRADUATES OF COLUMBUS MEDICAL COLLEGE.

Adams, C. W., '80 ..... Pennsylvania
Adams, W. T., '79 .... Ohio
Adsit, A. M., '81 .... New York
Agler, H. L., '78 .... Ohio
Alban, S. N., '79 .... Ohio
Albery, T. W., '77 .... Ohio
Anderson, J. R., '84 .... Ohio
Armstrong, F. C., A. B., '82 ... Ohio
Ashbrook. B. B., '82 .... Ohio
Ashbrook, Mahlon, '82 .... Ohio
Atkinson, R. E., '86 .... Ohio
Baker, C. E., '81 .... Ohio
Bancroft, J. L., '81 .... Ohio
Barker, Clark, '83 .... Ohio
Barnes, W. F., '83 .... Ohio
Barnhill, J. U., B. S., '83 .... Ohio
Barnett, C. L. V., '89 .... Ohio
Barton, R. S., '84 .... Ohio
Bates, C., '81 .... Michigan
Battles, W. S., '78 .... Ohio
Beall, J. A., '89 .... Ohio
Bebout, W. S., '80 .... Ohio
Beekman, J. J., '76 .... Ohio
Beggs, R. P., '88 ...... Pennsylvania
Bingham, J. T. '80 .... Ohio
Birchmore, W. H., A. B., '82. Kansas
Bird, E. H., '87 .... Ohio
Birmingham, J. W., '90 .... Ohio
Blake, F. W., A. B., '83 .... Ohio
Blake, H. C., '76 .... Ohio
Blakeley, G. W., '78 .... Ohio
Bland, J., '78 .... Ohio
Blose, J. U., '80 .... Pennsylvania
Bonheim, B. A., '82 .... Ohio
Boone, D. W., '83 .... Ohio

Bowman, J. C., '90 .... Ohio
Bowman, J. H., '90 .... Ohio
*Boyd, H. J., '79 .... Ohio
Boyd, H. M., '77 .... Ohio
*Boyd, W. M., '83 .... Ohio
Boylan, J. L., '87 .... Ohio
Bradford, J. J., '79 .... Ohio
Brady, W. B., '82 ..... Pennsylvania
Brainard, I. M., '81 .... Michigan
Brattain, G. M., '90 .... Ohio
Brown, C. E., B. S., '87 .... Ohio
Brown, J. S., '89 .... Ohio
Brown, R. S., '83 .... Ohio
Bryan, L. D., '78 .... Obio
Bryner, J. H., '85 ...... Pennsylvania
Brush, E. C., '76 .... Ohio
Bunn, W. S., '84 .... Ohio
Burns, E. E., '90 .... Ohio
Burr, W. A., '83 ..... Massachusetts
Byall, W. A., '78 .... Ohio
Campbell, F. W., '86 .... Ohio
Campbell, H. G., '82 .... Ohio
Campbell, H. J., '87 ... West Virginia
Carey, M. J., '82 .... New York
Carey, R. E. W., '79 .... Ohio
Carlisle, W. M., '84 .... Ohio
Chambers, R. P., '77 .... Ohio
Chesney, J. A., '79. .... Ohio
Chidester, C. W., B. S., '90 ..... Ohio
Clark, A. B., '90 .... Ohio
Clark, J. A., '81 .... Ohio
Clark, W. R., '81 .... Ohio
Clayson, L. T., '76 .... Ohio
Clewell, H. M., '76 .... Ohio
Clinger, J. A., '82 .... Ohio

Close, G. A., '76.............Ohio
Clouse, G. M., '90.............Ohio
Clutter, T. H. B., '79 ....Ohio
Cole, J. H., '89 ....Kansas
*Coleman, M. W., '76 ....Ohio
Coleman, J. H., '83 ....Ohio
Collins, J. M., '79·.............Ohio
Colvill, G. H., '79 ....Ohio
Comer, C. M., '82 ....Ohio
Comfort, R. P., '82..............Ohio
Connelly, W. A., '76...........Ohio
*Cook, E. R., '76 ....Ohio
Coons, C. S., '78...............Ohio
Cooper, Albert, '77..........Kansas
Costello, J. F., '80.....Pennsylvania
Cowles, A. L., '78.....Pennsylvania
Cowles, G. E., '89 ....Ohio
Craft, E. A., '77...............Ohio
Crane, A. M., '80..............Ohio
Crane, M., '78.............Indiana
Crawford, John, '87............Ohio
Crawford. J. M., '77 ....Ohio
Cromley, Harry, '82...........Ohio
Crow, J. H., '83.... ....Ohio
Cunningham, A. J., '88 .... Ohio
Custer, G. D., '84.............Ohio
Danforth, C. E., '80...........Ohio
Daugherty, L. E., '79 ....Ohio
Davenport, A. B., '90 ....Ohio
Davidson, N. P., '82...........Ohio
Davis, E. B., '86 ....Ohio
Davis, J. F., '84 ....Ohio
Davis, J. S., '78 ....Ohio
Davison, C. C., '77 ....Ohio
Dawson, F. J., '81 ....Ohio
Dawson, W. G., '81........ .. Ohio
Deemer, H. E., '83...........Ohio
Deeren, M. F., '87...........Ohio
Dent, A. M., '82.......West Virginia
Denman, J. K., '76 ....Ohio

Deuble, L. E., '86 .... Ohio
Dibert, C. C., '84 .... Pennsylvania
Dickie, A. D., '90 ....Pennsylvania
Dickinson, H. J., '82 .....New York
Dolan, W. K., '79 ....Ohio
Drake, S. S., '77..............Ohio
Drake, W. M., '81·...........Ohio
*Draper, Charles, '82·........ Ohio
Driscoll, P. B., '86·...........Ohio
Duff, J. S., '81..................Ohio
Dumbauld, D. F., '83.........Ohio
Dumm, A. W., '76.............Ohio
Dunham, C. C., '85 ....Ohio
Dunlap, C. O., '78.............Ohio
*Dye, G. W., '76 ....Ohio
*Edelman, S. F., '81...........Ohio
Egan, J. F., '82.. .... Ohio
Eigholz, A. M., '86 .... Ohio
Elder, J. T., '90 ....Ohio
Ellsworth, H. E., '82 .... Ohio
Elsbree, J. C., '89 ....Ohio
Emery, G. A., '79 ....Ohio
England, W. L., '81..........Ohio
English. G. F., '81 .... Indiana
*Evans, Frank, '83........... Ohio
*Evans, J. J., '83 ....Ohio
Evans, M. H., '84 ....Ohio
Eyman, H. C., '80.............Ohio
Faber, Wm., '89 .... Ohio
Falor, O. N., '83..............Ohio
Fisher, E. T., '80.............Ohio
Fleming, J. D., '87 ....Ohio
Fletcher, H. E., '87..........Ohio
*Follett, G. P., '79 ....Ohio
Forbes, R. S., '78.............Ohio
Foreman, A. J., '81·..........Ohio
Foster, W. A., '84.............Ohio
Francis, J. A., '79·............Ohio
Fruth, David, '79.............Ohio
Fulwider, R. M., '81..........Ohio

* Deceased.

Funderburg, Jesse, '86 ....Ohio
Furniss, H. A., '76 ....Ohio
*Gallogly, Wesley, '85.....Missouri
Gardiner, J. D., '79.........Illinois
Gardner, H. E., '89 .... Ohio
Gehring, H. F., '84 ....Ohio
Gerhardt, J. H., '82............Ohio
Gibson, J. M., '79..............Ohio
Gilliam, C. F., '78 ....Ohio
Gilmore, M. S., '83 ....Ohio
Glenn, L. G., '77 ....Ohio
Good, J. F., '80................Ohio
Gordon, J. W., '81.............Ohio
Gordon, T. G., '84.............Ohio
Gorselene, V. H., '77..........Ohio
Gossett, W. E., '89..........Kansas
Goudy, S. B., '81 ....Ohio
Graham, R. H., '79............Ohio
Gray, J. T., '79.......Pennsylvania
Gray, R. A., '82 ....Ohio
Green, W. J., '81..............Ohio
Greene, Chas., '79 ....Delaware
Gregg, M., '81 ....Ohio
Griffin, A. E., '84 ....Ohio
Griffin, J. K., '78 ....Ohio
Graves, J. E., '80..............Ohio
Hageman, J. A., '84...Pennsylvania
Hamer, J. W., '82.....Pennsylvania
Hamilton, C. S., A. B., '87......Ohio
Hamilton, J. L., '81...........Ohio
Hamilton, L. D., '81..........Ohio
Hamilton, S. S., '78....Pennsylvania
Hamilton, W. D., A. B., '83 ...Ohio
Hammond, W. A., '81....New York
Hanley, J. M., '77 ....Ohio
*Hanna, W. K., '82............Ohio
Hansen, R. W., '86 ....Ohio
Hanson, H. H., '81..New Brunswick
Hardy, J. G., '81 ....Ohio
Hardy, J. M., '77...............Ohio

Hardy, M. V. (Hon.), '80.......Ohio
Harper, E. D., '89............ Ohio
Harper, L. A., '84............Ohio
Harris. E. C., '76..............Ohio
Harris, J. W., '78..............Ohio
Harrison, C. B., '84 ....Ohio
Harrison, J. A., 85............Ohio
Hart, C. S., '77 .... Ohio
*Harter, W. B., '82 ....Ohio
Hartman, H. H., '90...........Ohio
Hatfield, W. E., '79 ....Ohio
Hayes, J. D., '78..............Ohio
Hayes, J. T., '80:..............Ohio
Hecker, E. A., '78............. Ohio
*Heckerman, W. H., '81.......Ohio
Hedrick, C. W., '83...........Ohio
Hempstead, C. B., '76 ....Ohio
Henderson, H. L., '84 ....Ohio
Henderson, Rob't, '80...W. Virginia
Hendrixson, O. P., '85.........Ohio
Henry, A. G., '87..............Ohio
Herbst, Edward, '84...........Ohio
Hershiser, H. K., '81 ....Ohio
Heston, J. Z., '89..............Ohio
Hewetson, W., '88.............Ohio
Hipple, J. R., '78..............Ohio
*Hirst, J. T., '83 ....Ohio
Hise, A. H., '79 ....Ohio
Hodges, W. C., '81............Ohio
Hoffhine, J. O., '77 ....Ohio
Holtz, J. M., '80...............Ohio
Homes, W. W., '77 ......New York
Hook, G. C., '85...............Ohio
Hoover, W. M., '80............Ohio
Hornby, J. W., '88 ....Ohio
Howe, J. F., '77 ....Ohio
Hoyt, H. F., '82.........Minnesota
Hughes, M. J., '77.............Ohio
*Hughes, J. H., '79............Ohio
Hughey, B., '80 ....Ohio

* Deceased.

Hughey, W. F., '80...........Ohio	Lawrence, J. C., '89...........Ohio
Humphreys, A., '82 ....Ohio	*Leahey, W. F., '76 ....Ohio
Hurd, A., '78................Ohio	Learned, A. J., '77...........Ohio
*Hutton, G. W., '78...........Ohio	Lee, W. B., '83...............Ohio
Hyde, R. L., D.D.S., '86 ......Ohio	Leech, J. A., Ph. B., '86.......Ohio
Hyde, W. F., '87.............Ohio	Leggett, W. A., '85...........Ohio
Iglick, Sam'l, '88. ....Ohio	Lewis, G. V., '89 ....Ohio
Imhoff, C. E., '83............Ohio	Light, Frank, '83 ....Ohio
Jackson, Alpha, '81...........Ohio	*Lindsay, S. D., '76..........Ohio
Jackson, A. L., '78 ....Ohio	Linn, W. I., '82 ....Ohio
Jackson, W. L., '90...........Ohio	Litten, W. B., '80............Ohio
Jacobs, P., B. S., '83..........Ohio	Lockwood. C. G., '88 ....Ohio
James, H. S., '90 ....Ohio	Longman, J. M., '84 ....Ohio
Jenkins, Wm., '84............Ohio	Lorimer, H. F., '83...........Ohio
Jewett, G. F., '82............Ohio	Lottridge, W. M., '80.........Ohio
Johnston, T. M., '82 ....Ohio	Lowe, J. W., '77..............Ohio
Jones, G. W., '79.............Ohio	Lupton, L. S., '87............Ohio
Jones, Ola S., '83............Ohio	Lynch, H. G., '78............Ohio
Jones, T. K., '83.............Ohio	*Lyons, A. W., '76 ....Ohio
Jump, J. S., '81..............Ohio	Lyons, J. W., '77 ....Ohio
Kackley, J. M., '82...........Ohio	McAlpine, A. M., '77.........Ohio
Keefer, A. H., '80............Ohio	McCafferty, C. S., '90.........Ohio
*Keesor, L. W., '80...........Ohio	McCall, J. C., '79............Ohio
Keller, D. H., '82.....Pennsylvania	*McCall, J. H., '78 ....Ohio
Kelley, F. L., '81...........Indiana	McCann, J., '79 ....Ohio
Kennon, M., '85..............Ohio	McCarey, M. J., B. S., '90.....Penn.
Keyes, L. W., '82.........Michigan	McClintock, A., '88...........Ohio
Kilgore, J. M., '82...........Ohio	McCormick, E. G., '79.........Ohio
King, L. J., '80.......Pennsylvania	McCormick, Richard, '84......Ohio
Kinkead, W. W., '82 ....Ohio	McCoy, H. F., '79............Ohio
Kinnaman, H. L., '83..........Ohio	McCrary, A. H., '83 ....Ohio
Kirby, F. M., '82............Ohio	McCurdy, S. L., '81 ....Ohio
Kirk, J. A., '83........Pennsylvania	McDaniel, B. E., '89..........Ohio
Kirkpatrick, C. F., '82........Ohio	McDonald, D. L., '81..Pennsylvania
Lane, B. E., '80 ....Ohio	McDonald, E., '82............Ohio
Lane, W. G., '86 ....Ohio	McKitrick, Llewellyn, '90.....Ohio
Lash, J. W., '78 ....Ohio	McMaster, R. O., '77..........Ohio
Lautenslager, J., '82..........Ohio	McMurray, J. C., '84.....Minnesota
Lawrence, A. E., '90 ....Ohio	McQueen, C. S., '78...........Ohio
Lawrence, F. F., '85..........Ohio	Macklin, F. M., '90...........Ohio

* Deceased.

Magers, A. M., '85 ....Ohio

Magrew, A., '78..............Ohio

Main, A. E., '79..............Ohio

*Major, J. M., '82 . ...Ohio

Mangus, G. W., '88 ......New York

Mann, L. H., '83 ············Ohio

Marchant, Grant, '87 ....Ohio

Marshall, G. M., '80..........Ohio

Marshall, J. C., '83 ....Ohio

Marshall, L. H., '77 ....Ohio

Martin, C. V., '82 ......New York

Mason, J. T., '81 ....Ohio

Masters, G. H., '77 ....Ohio

Matthias, L. A., '79...........Ohio

Mauk, P. P., '90. ....Ohio

Medbery, Josiah, A. B., '78 ....Ohio

Merryman, R. M., '81 ....Ohio

Michaels, A. L., '81........Indiana

Miles, G. W., '79........ New York

Miller, D. H., '84.............Ohio

Miller, H. W., '78............Ohio

Miller, R. B., '80 ....Ohio

Miller, T. J., '78.............Ohio

Miller, W. R., '76 ....Indiana

Millhouse, G. R., '78 ....Ohio

Mills, J. T., '81 ....Ohio

*Miner, A. G., '81 ....Ohio

Mitchell, W. F., '76 ....Ohio

Montgomery, C. R., '80........Ohio

Moore, F. R., '85.............Ohio

Moore, H. M. W., A.B., '85· .. Ohio

Morehouse, G. W., '86..].....Ohio

Morgan, J. F., '81 ....Ohio

Mouser, A. H., '89......... ... Ohio

Munson, L. D., '81.... ......Ohio

Murphy, J. A., '90............Ohio

Nelson, J. W., '77.............Ohio

Nesbit, J. C., '81......Pennsylvania

Newell, S. C., '80· . ...Iowa

Niswanger, H. L., '85.........Ohio

Niswanger, M., '79 ....Ohio

Nye, O. S., '81............New York

O'Brine, David, B.S., M.E., '85..Ohio

Olmstead, W. H., '90·.Pennsylvania

Ong, A. R., '77................Ohio

Osbourne, G. W., '83.........Ohio

Ott, C. W. G., '79 ....Ohio

Ottwell, C. W., '76 ....Ohio

Ottwell, E. S., '76.............Ohio

*Owen, I. P., '82 ....Ohio

Paine, D. L., '78......Pennsylvania

Parker, C. M., '90...........Ohio

Parker, F. H., '80 ....Ohio

Parkinson, L. A., '87 ....Ohio

Parsons, E. E., '88 ....Ohio

Patchen, F. J., '81..........Indiana

Pattin, T. B., '78..... ....Ohio

Pearce, H. M., '90...........Ohio

Pheneger, P. W., '82..........Ohio

Phillips, D. W., '85 ....:...Ohio

Phillips, G. A., '90 ....Ohio

Phillips, W. S., '82...........Ohio

Plumer, J. J., '82 ....Iowa

Pollinger, R. B., '83...Pennsylvania

Pounds, A. J., '81·........... Ohio

Powell, D. J., '76 ....Ohio

Pratt, B. W., '82..............Ohio

Pratt, Laura M., '84...........Ohio

Preston, H. S., '76.............Ohio

Prose, T. W., '84 ....Ohio

Radebaugh, H. A., '76.........Ohio

Randall, W. C. J., '81.. ....Ohio

Rankin, T. W., '77...........Ohio

Rea, M. M., '81...............Ohio

Reynolds, F. A., '79........Indiana

Reynolds, J. F., '87............Ohio

Rhodes, J. M., '88............Ohio

Richards, O. B., '82..... New York

Richards, S. S., '79............Ohio

Richardson, E. O., '84........Ohio

* Deceased.

Richey, G. W., '83 ....Ohio
Richey, R. C., '82............Ohio
Ridgeway, N. B., '77.........Ohio
Riley, C., '81 ....Ohio
Riley, W., '81................Ohio
*Riley, W. A., '83.............Ohio
Robertson, J., '81 ....Ohio
Robinson, S. R., '78.......Indiana
*Rockwell, J. J., '82 ....Ohio
Rosengrant, C. L., '90........Ohio
Rosengrant, T. S., '83 ....Ohio
Rowles, W. T., '81...........Ohio
Royce, W. T., '82 ....Illinois
*Rudolph, J. W., '77..........Ohio
Rugh, W. J., '77.............Ohio
Sager, A. H., '78.............Ohio
Sager, C. F., '84..............Ohio
Sager, F. P., '80..............Ohio
*Sams, A. B., '79 ....Ohio
Sarbaugh, M. F., '86 ....Ohio
*Schooley, C., '78............Ohio
Schug, F. J., '76 ....Ohio
Schultze, H. L., '83 ...Pennsylvania
Scofield, L. F., '81............Ohio
Scott, C. A., '87..............Ohio
Scott, W. C., '90..............Ohio
*Scott, J. P., '81..............Ohio
Sears, O. T., '82..............Ohio
Shanks, M. L., '82.........Dakota
Sharp, B. M., '79.............Ohio
Sharp, B. M., '84.............Iowa
Sharp, P. H., '84.............Iowa
Shattuck, Wm., '82..........Ohio
Shaw, O. J., '90 ....Ohio
Sheadel, W. T., '82...Pennsylvania
Sheckler, C. R., '78...........Ohio
Shoemaker, W. W., '78.......Ohio
Shook, J. W., '85.............Ohio
Smith, A. F., '78.............Ohio
Smith, H. B., '77..............Ohio

Smith, H. L., '78 ....Ohio
Smith, G., '79 ....Ohio
Smith, J. A., '89 ....Ohio
Smith, O. J., '82 ....Ohio
Smith, S. G., '78..............Ohio
*Smith, Wm., '76 ....Ohio
Smith, Wm. H., '80 ....Ohio
Spaulding, C. F., '86. ....Ohio
Sprague, M. H., '80 ....Ohio
Spring, N. C., '77 ....Ohio
Squires, A. W., '83...........Iowa
Squires, D. H., '80·........Missouri
Stallard, H. H., '90.........Virginia
Steel, R. M., '81 ....Ohio
Steen, W. D., '83 ....Ohio
Sterrett, J. A., '78 ....Ohio
Stevenson, A. G., '79.......Indiana
Stewart, F. M., '83...........Ohio
Stickney, F. A., '80...........Ohio
Stockton, M. L., '87.......Kansas
Stokes, W. H., '82.............Ohio
Stonehocker, W. W., '81......Ohio
Strayer, F. P., '79 ....Ohio
Strecker, J. J., '80.............Ohio
Summers, N. P., '87..........Iowa
Swearingen, S. P., '83......Kansas
Talbot, T. M., A.B., '88.......Ohio
Taylor, H. M., '82.....Pennsylvania
Taylor, J. B., '81............Ohio
Taylor, Wilson, '80........Kansas
Theiss, H. C., '86 ....Ohio
Thomen, A. A., '81·..........Ohio
Thompson, F. E., '88 ....Ohio
*Thompson, J. H., '76........Ohio
Thrailkill, G. H., '83 ....Ohio
Townsley, J. C., '89...........Ohio
Traster, W. H. H., '89........Ohio
Trimble, T. W., '78 ....Ohio
Trovinger, J. R., '89·.........Ohio
Trovinger, M. S., '83.........Ohio

*Deceased.

Tupper, C. G., '82.............Ohio
*Tuppins, Isaiah, '84.... .....Ohio
Valentine, V. A., '76...........Ohio
Vanfossan, J. M., '83 ....Ohio
Vansant, W. P., '80·........Indiana
Vernard, W. M., '78........Kansas
Vernier, L. A., '89.............Ohio
Vickers, H. A., '84............Ohio
Vigor, F. A., '79..............Ohio
Vigor, J. F., '79..............Ohio
Vigor, W. C., '84............. Ohio
Vogt, J. W. N., '76..`........Ohio
Wagley, S. L., '78 ....Ohio
Wagner, H. M., '79............Ohio
Walcott, O. N., '79............Ohio
Walker, A. E., '80..........,....Ohio
Walker, R. J., '85.............Ohio
Wallace, J. M., '79.........Illinois
Wallace, W. F., '80......Michigan
Wallace, W. R., '80...........Ohio
Warner, Wm., '79·.........Indiana
Warren, L., '78·...............Ohio
Warren, W. W., '89...........Ohio
Waters, W. C., '82·.........;..Ohio
Watkins, C. D., '86............Ohio
*Watkins, J. S., '77...........Ohio
Watters, S. C., '81.............Ohio
Weaver, D. S., '80...........Ohio
Webb, W. J., '84...........Illinois
Weeks, O. W., '76,............Ohio

Welker, A. E., '81............Ohio
Whitcomb, E. H., '84....Minnesota
Whittaker, Dennis, '83........Ohio
Whitten, Wm., '86...........Ohio
Wickham, W. H., '82........ Ohio
*Wight, A. C., '79..Sandwich Islands
Wilkin, C. F., '82.............Ohio
Wilkins, J. A., '78 ....Ohio
Williams, E. A., '88 ....Ohio
Williams, J. H., '85...........Ohio
Williamson, G. H., '78........Ohio
Willis, A. M., '82.............Ohio
Wilson, J. F., '81.............Ohio
Wilson, T. R., '79............Ohio
Wilson, W. A.. '78 ....Ohio
Wirt, M. O., '78.............. Ohio
Wise, S. L., '84...............Ohio
Wolfe, A. C., '83 ....Ohio
Wolfe, J. H., '77. .... Ohio
Wood, J. M., '79 ....Ohio
Wood, W. F., '76.............Ohio
Workman, J. C., '79 ....Ohio
Wright, T. B., A. B., '86 .....Ohio
Wyant, W. J., '89.............Ohio
Wylie, S. J., '87 ....Ohio
Yarnell, F. H., '79............Ohio
Yeater, S. H., '88.............Ohio
Young, H. H., '90 ....Ohio
Young, O. R., '84.............Ohio
Zulch, Gustav, '76 ....Germany

Lectures on Insanity.

D. A. MORSE, M. D.,

Superintendent of the Columbus Asylum for the Insane, and formerly Professor of *Mental Diseases* in Columbus Medical College, has kindly agreed to deliver a course of lectures on Insanity and allied Mental and Nervous Diseases. These lectures will be most abundantly illustrated by the almost unlimited supply of cases furnished by the Asylum.

Rapid transportation to the Asylum is available.

THE HAWKES HOSPITAL

CPSIA information can be obtained
at www.ICGtesting.com
Printed in the USA
BVHW041757301118
534322BV00030B/262/P